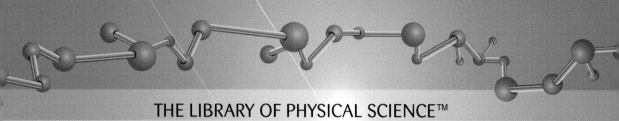

THE LIBRARY OF PHYSICAL SCIENCE™

Elements in Living Organisms

Suzanne Slade

The Rosen Publishing Group's

PowerKids Press™

New York

To Jack and Sophie Reposa

Published in 2007 by The Rosen Publishing Group, Inc.
29 East 21st Street, New York, NY 10010

First Edition

Editor: Amelie von Zumbusch
Book Design: Elana Davidian
Layout Design: Ginny Chu
Photo Researcher: Gabriel Caplan

Photo Credits: Cover, p. 12 © David Aubrey/Corbis; p. 4 © Ariel Skelley/Corbis; p. 5 © Susumu Nishinaga/Photo Researchers, Inc.; p. 6 © Charles D. Winters/Photo Researchers, Inc.; p. 8 NASA Goddard Space Flight Center; p. 10 © Véronique Estiot/Photo Researchers, Inc.; p. 11 © Pete Atkinson/The Image Bank/Getty Images; p. 13 © AJPhoto/Photo Researchers, Inc.; p. 14 © Dr. Kari Lounatmaa/Photo Researchers, Inc.; p. 15 © Ralph Clevenger/Corbis; p. 16 © First/zefa/Corbis; p. 17 © SERCOMI/Photo Researchers, Inc.; p. 18 Stephen Ausmus/USDA; p. 19 www.istockphoto.com/ Dan Brandenburg; p. 20 Cindy Reiman; p. 21 © Norbert Schaefer/Corbis.

Library of Congress Cataloging-in-Publication Data

Slade, Suzanne.
   Elements in living organisms / Suzanne Slade.— 1st ed.
      p. cm. — (The library of physical science)
   ISBN 1-4042-3424-1 (library binding) — ISBN 1-4042-2171-9 (pbk.)
   1. Chemical elements—Juvenile literature. 2. Biology—Juvenile literature. I. Title. II. Series.
QD466.S563 2007
572—dc22
                                                                    2005033443

Manufactured in the United States of America

Contents

A World of Organisms

How are you like a dog, a grasshopper, and a flower? A dog, a grasshopper, a flower, and you are all organisms. An organism is anything that is living. Every person, animal, and plant is an organism. Organisms live in trees, lakes, caves, houses, and even under the ground. The world is filled with millions of different organisms.

Organisms are made of tiny parts called cells. Cells join together in

This boy, his dog, and the plants around them are organisms. The sand in the road is not an organism, because it is not alive.

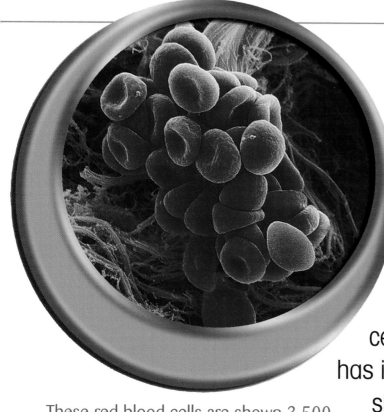

different ways to form all living things. Cells are so small you cannot see them.
Your body has many different cells. Each cell has its own job. Your skin is made of flat cells. They fit together like

These red blood cells are shown 3,500 times larger than their real size. Red blood cells carry oxygen around the body.

pieces in a puzzle to keep your body safe. The cells in your **muscles** get longer and shorter to help you move. The millions of blood cells in your body carry **oxygen**. Organisms need cells to grow and stay alive.

Common Elements in Organisms

Tiny parts called atoms make up everything in the world, including organisms. There are more than 100 different kinds of atoms. An element is matter that is made of only one kind of atom. For example, iron is an element. A piece of iron is made only of iron atoms.

Carbon is an element found in all organisms. Three other elements that are commonly found in organisms are oxygen, **hydrogen**, and **nitrogen**. More than 96 percent of your body is made of carbon, oxygen, hydrogen, and nitrogen.

Every element has a **symbol** of one, two, or three letters. The symbols for carbon, oxygen,

Carbon, shown at right, is often found as a soft, gray solid.

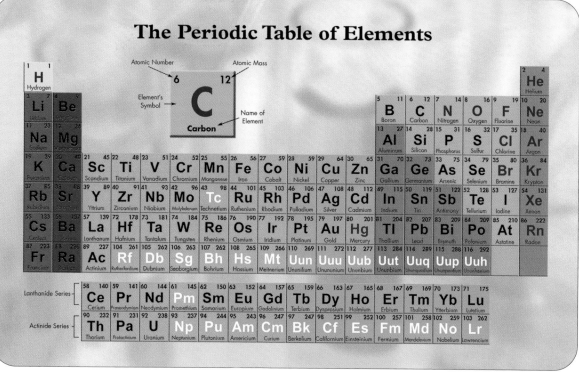

The periodic table, shown above, lists all the known elements. Carbon, oxygen, nitrogen, and hydrogen are near the top of the table.

hydrogen, and nitrogen are the first letter of their names. For example, carbon's symbol is C. All elements are listed on a chart called the periodic table. Hydrogen is in the first row on the periodic table. Carbon, nitrogen, and oxygen are all in the second row.

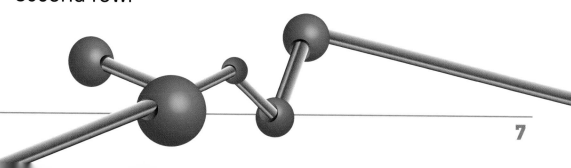

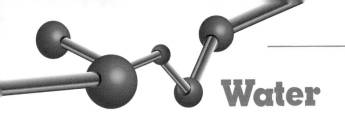

Water

Sometimes atoms of different elements combine to create **compounds**. Water is the most important compound for life on Earth. It covers more than 70 percent of Earth's surface. More than half of your body is made of water. You could live only about one week without water. All organisms need water to live.

Water is created when two hydrogen atoms and one

Earth is covered with so much water that it looks mostly blue from space.

Hydrogen atoms have one electron. Oxygen atoms have eight electrons. Two hydrogen atoms and one oxygen atom share electrons in a water molecule.

oxygen atom join together. The **formula** for water is H_2O. The small two after the H means there are two atoms of hydrogen in one **molecule** of water. The single O stands for one atom of oxygen.

$$H_2 \quad + \quad O \quad \Rightarrow \quad H_2O$$

hydrogen   oxygen   water

A bond is formed between hydrogen and oxygen because the hydrogen atoms share **electrons** with the oxygen atom. This type of bond is called a covalent bond.

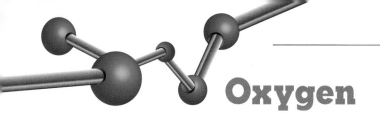

Oxygen

Take a deep breath. What are you breathing in? If you said oxygen, you are partly right. The air you breathe is about 21 percent oxygen gas. Air also has other gases, such as nitrogen, in it. Oxygen has no color, odor, or taste. Without thinking about it, you breathe in air all the time. Your lungs take in oxygen from the air and then pass the oxygen into your blood. Blood is a purple color when it is low in oxygen. After

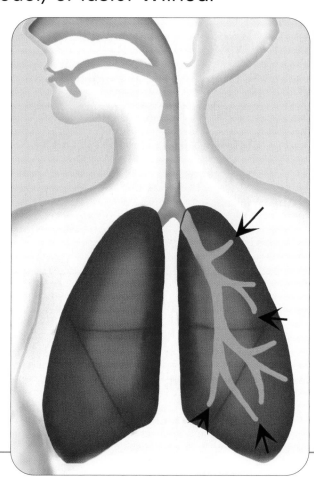

The air you breathe in moves down a tube called the windpipe and into your lungs. There blood takes in oxygen from the air.

People who dive deep under water use oxygen tanks so that they can breathe even though there is no air.

blood gets oxygen from the lungs, it becomes bright red. Blood takes oxygen to your body's cells. Your cells use oxygen to make energy. Energy is the power to work or to act.

Oxygen atoms tend to join up in pairs. Two oxygen atoms combine to form one molecule of oxygen. An oxygen molecule is shown by the formula O_2. The bond between oxygen atoms is a covalent bond.

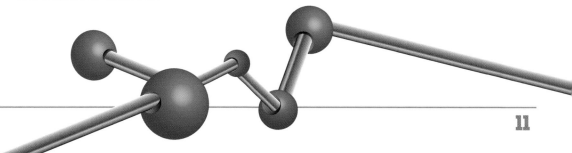

Nitrogen

All living organisms need nitrogen. Your body uses nitrogen in many ways. For example, nitrogen is needed to build muscles. It also helps your body grow hair and skin cells.

As oxygen atoms do, nitrogen atoms often pair together. The formula for a nitrogen molecule is N_2. A molecule of nitrogen gas is formed from two nitrogen atoms. The nitrogen atoms are joined by covalent

Plants depend on their roots to take in nitrogen from the soil.

bonds. The two nitrogen atoms share three different pairs of electrons.

Nitrogen is all around you, but you cannot see it. You do not smell it either, because nitrogen has no odor. The air is 78 percent nitrogen gas. However, your body cannot get nitrogen from the air.

People get the nitrogen they need from the food they eat.

All nitrogen in organisms comes from the soil. Plants take in nitrogen through their roots. You get nitrogen by eating plants or animals that have eaten plants.

Carbon Dioxide

Do you know your body creates something plants need? When you breathe out, you give off carbon dioxide gas. Plants need carbon dioxide to grow and live. Plants use carbon dioxide to make the oxygen you need.

Photosynthesis happens in parts of plant cells called chloroplasts. The chloroplasts above are many times their real size.

Carbon dioxide is made of two elements, carbon and oxygen. Its formula is CO_2.

C	+	O_2	$\Rightarrow$	CO_2
carbon		oxygen		carbon dioxide

People depend on plants to make the oxygen we need to live. The plants above grow in the rainforest.

One molecule of carbon dioxide is created when one carbon atom combines with two oxygen atoms. The two oxygen atoms are joined to the carbon atom by covalent bonds. The carbon and oxygen atoms share electrons.

Plants use CO_2 in **photosynthesis**. During photosynthesis, plants use sunlight, carbon dioxide, and water to make oxygen and sugar called glucose. Plants need **glucose** for energy to grow.

$$\text{sunlight} + 6CO_2 + 6H_2O \Rightarrow C_6H_{12}O_6 + 6O_2$$

| | carbon dioxide | water | | sugar | | oxygen |

A Sugar Called Glucose

Carbon, hydrogen, and oxygen combine to form sugar. When you see the word sugar, you probably think of the white grains you put on cereal. However, there are many kinds of sugar. White table sugar is called sucrose. Fructose is a sugar found in fruits. The sugar in milk is called lactose.

Your body uses another type of sugar called glucose. Glucose is found in some of the foods you

About half the table sugar in the United States is made from sugar beets, shown at right.

The yellow shapes above are the parts of a human cell that use glucose to make energy. They are shown at many times their real size.

eat, such as vegetables. Your **liver** and muscles also make glucose from other foods. A molecule of glucose sugar has 6 carbon atoms, 12 hydrogen atoms, and 6 oxygen atoms. Its formula is $C_6H_{12}O_6$. The six carbon atoms are joined together in the center of this large molecule. Each carbon atom bonds to carbon, hydrogen, and oxygen atoms. The cells in your body use glucose and oxygen to give you energy.

$$C_6H_{12}O_6 \; + \; 6O_2 \; \Rightarrow \; 6CO_2 \; + \; 6H_2O \; + \; energy$$

glucose   oxygen   carbon dioxide   water

The Carbon Cycle

Carbon can be found in every living organism. It is also present in the air and soil. Carbon atoms join easily with other atoms to form carbon compounds. Plants and animals need carbon compounds to grow and live.

Carbon atoms move through nature in a cycle. A cycle is a pattern that happens again and again. The carbon cycle begins when plants

When cows eat grass they are taking carbon into their bodies in the form of sugars like glucose.

Plants, such as the corn above, take in carbon from the carbon dioxide from the air.

take carbon dioxide from the air and create glucose, a carbon compound. When animals eat plants, they take carbon from the glucose, which is a carbon compound, into their bodies. The glucose gives them energy. As animals breathe and give off carbon dioxide, the carbon inside their bodies goes back into the air. Carbon also leaves animals when they die. When animals' bodies decay, or rot, carbon dioxide goes into the air, and some carbon from the bodies goes into the earth. The carbon cycle starts again when plants take carbon dioxide from the air.

Hydrocarbons

Compounds that are made from hydrogen and carbon are called hydrocarbons. There are thousands of different hydrocarbons. Some hydrocarbons, such as plant oils, are found in foods. The red color in tomatoes and watermelons comes from hydrocarbons. Other hydrocarbons form deep inside the earth. Over time the bodies of organisms that have died sink down into the earth. After millions of years, these bodies become hydrocarbons, such as oil and natural gas.

Hydrocarbons are often used for

The wax that honeybees make is about 10% to 15% hydrocarbons.

This power plant in Germany burns the hydrocarbon coal.

fuels. Gas for cars is made from the hydrocarbon oil. Special factories called power plants burn hydrocarbons, like oil and coal, to make electricity for our homes. The simplest hydrocarbon is methane gas. Methane gas has one carbon atom and four hydrogen atoms. Natural gas is made of methane gas. People use natural gas to heat their homes. Propane, another hydrocarbon, is burned in gas grills.

Compounds that include carbon are called organic compounds. Some fuels, like natural gas and oil, are organic compounds. Your body makes other organic compounds, such as glucose. Scientists can combine elements in a lab to create compounds called synthetic compounds. Synthetic compounds made with carbon, such as plastic milk jugs and ketchup bottles, are an important part of your life. Your sneakers are made of synthetic compounds like rubber, glue, and nylon.

All organisms have carbon, oxygen, hydrogen, and nitrogen in them. These elements combine in different ways to create compounds that organisms need. Organisms around the world are connected by the elements they share.

Glossary

compounds (KOM-powndz) Matter made of atoms of more than one element joined together.

electrons (ih-LEK-tronz) Parts inside atoms that spin around the nucleus. They have a negative charge.

formula (FAWR-myuh-luh) A group of symbols and numbers that show what is in a compound or molecule.

fuels (FYOOLZ) Things used to make energy, warmth, or power.

glucose (GLOO-kohs) The sugar that the body uses for energy.

hydrogen (HY-droh-jen) A colorless gas that burns easily and weighs less than any other known element.

liver (LIH-ver) The part of the body that makes and stores glucose.

molecule (MAH-lih-kyool) Two or more atoms joined together.

muscles (MUH-sulz) Parts of the body that can be tightened or loosened to make the body move.

nitrogen (NY-truh-jen) A gas without taste, color, or odor, which can be found in the air.

oxygen (OK-sih-jen) A gas that has no color, taste, or odor and is necessary for people and animals to breathe.

photosynthesis (foh-toh-SIN-thuh-sus) The way in which green plants make their own food from sunlight, water, and carbon dioxide.

symbol (SIM-bul) The letter or letters that stand for an element.

Index

Web Sites

Due to the changing nature of Internet links, PowerKids Press has developed an online list of Web sites related to the subject of this book. This site is updated regularly. Please use this link to access the list:

www.powerkidslinks.com/lops/organisms/